LAURA SOFIE HANTKE   LUCAS GRASSMANN

Kitchen Lithography

——  ——

HAND PRINTING AT HOME

——— ✺ ———

FROM BUTTONS AND BAGS
TO POSTCARDS AND PILLOWCASES

Princeton Architectural Press
New York

CONTENTS

Hello and welcome to our kitchen!

We love handprinted treasures, the smell of printing ink, the feel of high-quality paper. As design students we had endless opportunities to make prints: from linoleum prints to etchings to screen printing. When the end of our studies neared, we realized that we would soon no longer have all these options. So we started looking for a printing method that would allow us to make high-quality prints without being tied to the equipment of a printing workshop.

In our search we came across "kitchen litho," a special printing method that was developed by the French artist Émilie Aizier–Brouard aka Emilion.

This technique, which is based on the principle of lithography, is fast, inexpensive, and completely non-toxic. What is fascinating about this method is that you probably have most of the materials needed already at home.

The printing plate is made of aluminum foil; plain vegetable oil replaces turpentine; and cola is used to etch the printing plate.

It sounds easy—and it is!—but when we first started experimenting with kitchen lithography, a lot of things went wrong. We learned from our mistakes, bad luck, and glitches, adjusted the technique to our creative needs, and further developed it for our purposes.

In this book we want to share what we learned—and the fun we had in the process—so you can enjoy printing from the start.

Have fun experimenting!
Laura and Lucas

ALL OF THE EXAMPLES ON THE
FOLLOWING PAGES ARE EXPLAINED
IN MORE DETAIL ON PAGES 106–110.

THE NUTS AND BOLTS

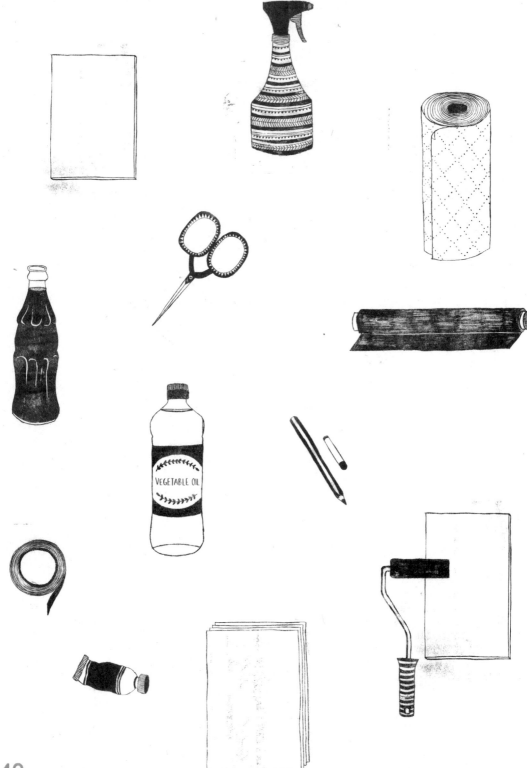

1

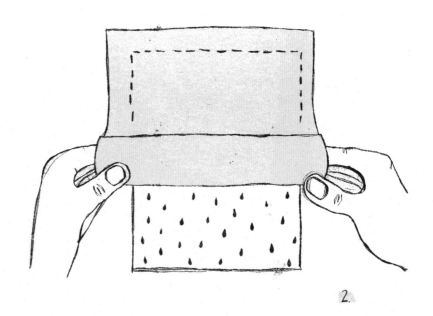

2

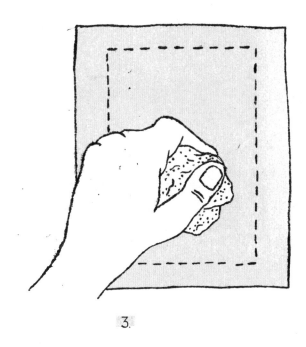

3.

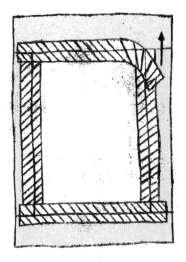

4.

STEP 2

DRAWING

WHAT YOU NEED:

Your printing plate
Oil pastels
Oil–based drawing pencils
Oil–based soap
Bowl of water
Paintbrush

aw your design on the printing plate as a mirror image,
ce it will be reversed when printed.

e lines in your drawing should be continuous, because
ey form a protective layer on the aluminum foil
d prevent etching at those points. Draw over the lines
second time to make sure there are no breaks.

e oil–based pencils to create fine lines, and oil pastels
soap and paintbrush for larger areas. Take a wet brush
d rub it over your piece of soap until the brush hairs
e all soapy, then paint your printing plate with it. Before
u proceed to the next step—etching—make sure to
the soap drawing dry completely; otherwise the soap
l spread over the printing plate, resulting in a fuzzy print.

You can use any oil–based materials to create your drawing. For example, we have also experimented with vegetable oil and brush, with the oil from our fingers, and even an oil–based face cream. You can also cut off a piece of soap and draw directly on the plate with it.

Most commercial soaps are oil–based, but you can also use gall soap or soft soap.

Keep the drawing simple for your first printing plate. In the beginning, we spent a lot of time on our drawings and then were rather disappointed when the printing plate didn't work.

Should the foil tear shortly after you've started to draw, go back to Step 1. If you've been working on your drawing for quite some time, go to page 78, in the "Troubleshooting" chapter, where we explain how you can still save your printing plate.

1

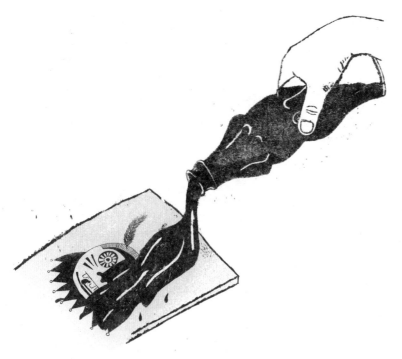

2.

3.

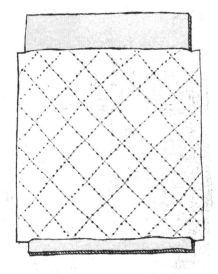

1

2.

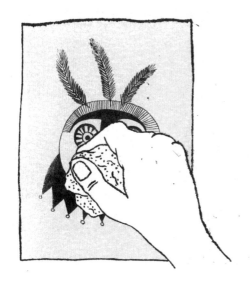

3.

4.

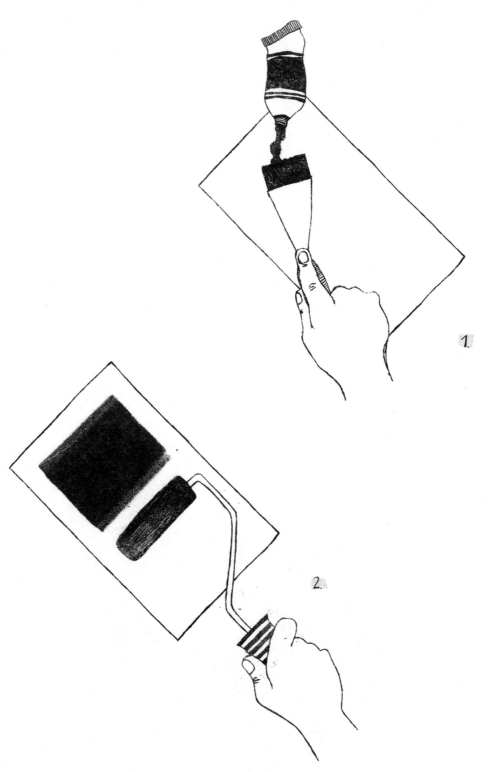

1.

2.

3.

4.

TIP

Use a cotton swab to ink small details of your drawing that are difficult to paint with the roller.

MULTICOLOR INKING + RAINBOW PRINTING

WHAT YOU NEED:

Your printing plate sprayed with water
Two different colors of oil–based paint
Surface for rolling out the paints
Two paint rollers
Spray bottle with water

1. You can also ink individual parts of your printing plate with different colors. Use a new paint roller for each color of paint. Carefully roll each roller over the parts of the design you want to ink with the respective color.

2. To print a progression, prepare your printing plate for inking as usual. Then ink two–thirds of your design with the lighter color. Roll out the darker color across the remaining third. You can now begin to mix both colors on the printing plate. To do this, take the roller with the darker color and carefully roll it from the darker color to the lighter color. Reduce the pressure on the roller gradually as you spread the paint into the lighter areas to achieve a smooth progression. Just experiment a bit to see what works best for your purposes.

1.

2.

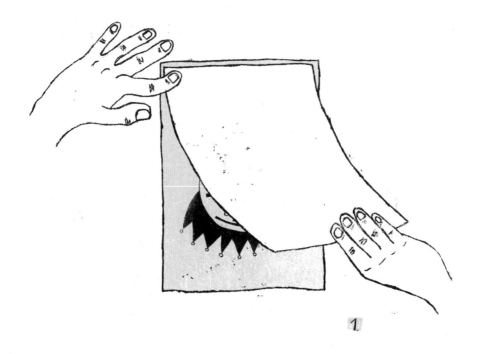

1.

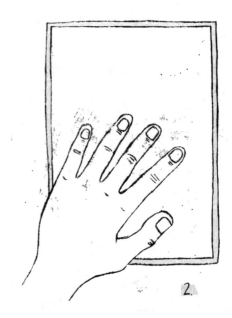

2.

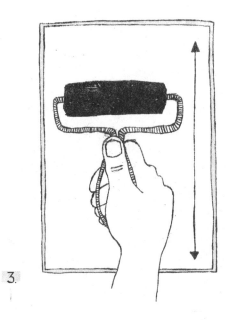

3.

4.

1/350

350/350

IF EVERYTHING GOES WELL, YOU CAN CREATE UP TO TWO
HUNDRED PRINTS FROM ONE PRINTING PLATE. THE
PRINTING PLATE WILL BECOME INCREASINGLY WORN AND
AT SOME POINT WILL START TO TAKE ON PAINT IN PLACES
WHERE THERE SHOULDN'T BE ANY. BUT SOMETIMES THIS
MAKES THE RESULTS EVEN MORE INTERESTING. WE PRINTED
A RUN OF 350 COPIES OF THE LITTLE GUY ABOVE. TO MAKE
THE PLATE MORE DURABLE WE FIRST COVERED IT WITH
GUM ARABIC. READ MORE ON HOW TO DO THIS ON PAGE 86
IN THE CHAPTER "ADDITIONAL TECHNIQUES."

PRINTING PLATE 1

PRINTING PLATE 2

58

PRINTING PLATE 1

PRINTING PLATE 2

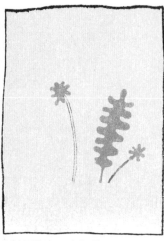

PRINTING PLATE 3

PRINTING PLATE 4

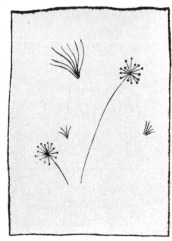

PRINTING PLATE 5

PRINTING PLATES 1 TO 3:
INKED WITH TWO COLORS

PRINTING PLATES 4 AND 5:
INKED WITH ONE COLOR

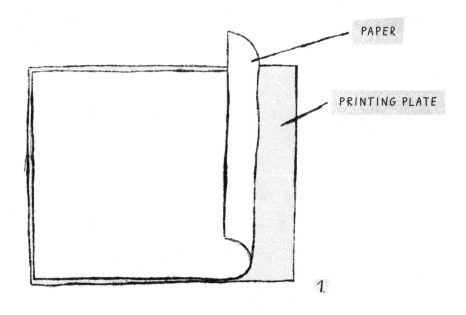

PAPER

PRINTING PLATE

1.

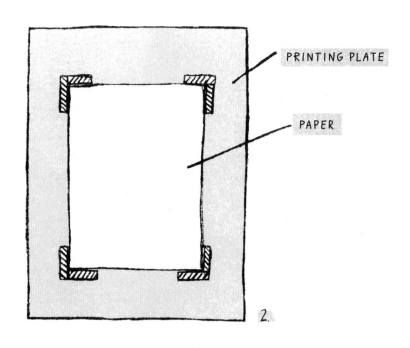

PRINTING PLATE

PAPER

2.

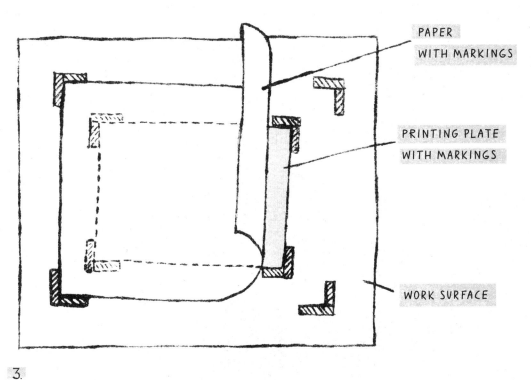

PAPER
WITH MARKINGS

PRINTING PLATE
WITH MARKINGS

WORK SURFACE

3.

WE MADE THIS PRINT USING A PRINTING PLATE
THAT STOOD NEXT TO OUR KITCHEN SINK FOR
OVER SIX MONTHS, WHERE IT WAS EXPOSED TO
SPLASHES OF WATER, GREASE, AND BATTER.

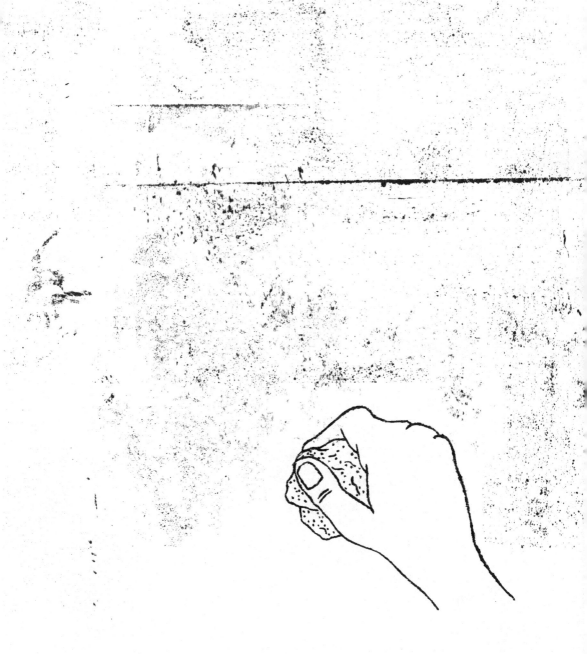

TROUBLESHOOTING

THE SMOKE RISING FROM
THE CHIMNEY IS THE RESULT
OF INTENTIONAL FINGERPRINTS.

FUZZY PRINT IMAGE

Fingerprints and other oily stains can easily end up on the printing plate and take on color during inking. We find this quite charming and often use this effect intentionally as a stylistic device. However, if you want a clear and clean print image, you can always just remove the paint adhering to these stains on the printing plate with a cotton swab before printing.

THE PRINT IS TOO DARK

You have probably applied too much paint. Just make sure to use less paint for the next printing. If the print still comes out too dark, wipe off all paint from the plate with a little vegetable oil and a paper towel and re-ink your plate. In addition, experiment with the pressure you apply to the paper when printing. You will quickly get the hang of it.

THE PRINT IS TOO LIGHT

You may not have applied enough paint to the plate or not enough pressure to the paper.

It is also possible that the printing plate was exposed to the cola for too long or that the drawing was applied too lightly. In those cases it is best to start over again from the beginning.

SPOON MARKS

If you use a spoon during printing, make sure to apply equal pressure all over. A good alternative is using a dry roller or simply the ball of your hand.

However, you can also play around with this "problem" and create special patterns by irregularly applying pressure of different degrees.

THE ETCHED AREA ABSORBS PAINT

If the printing plate takes on paint at places where there is no drawing, make sure that the whole plate is sufficiently covered with water before inking it.

The paint may also make streaks in the water. If this occurs, it means that you did not remove all of the vegetable oil. Just wipe paint and water off again with a little oil and then rinse the plate until all of the oil has washed off. Cover the plate with water again, before you start applying the paint.

However, if you like the effect and want to use it as a stylistic device, you know what you need to do.

If the etched area absorbs paint even though there was no leftover oil on the printing plate and you did not forget to run water over it, simply wipe off the undesired paint with a wet sponge. With a little luck, these places will not take on any paint the next time you ink the plate.

If you have already made some prints and the printing plate has slowly gotten dirty, try replacing the paint roller attachment. Sometimes that works wonders.

WHAT WE LEARNED DURING THE WARM SUMMER DAYS WHEN WE WERE WORKING ON FINISHING THIS BOOK:

For three days nothing worked. We constantly ended up with patterns in the etched areas when inking the plates. We took apart each individual step, did everything differently, and even bought new materials. Finally, we realized it could be because of the hot weather. So we put the aluminum foil in the freezer for a couple of hours. At 2:30 am on the third cursed day, we prepared the printing plate with the aluminum foil from the freezer. And lo and behold, the printing plate worked without any problems.

TEARS AND HOLES IN THE ALUMINUM FOIL

Sometimes the aluminum foil tears a little when you draw on it. Usually this is the case when the glass plate is not completely clean: the pencil gets stuck at an uneven spot under the aluminum foil and tears it there.

However, don't despair. In most cases you do not need to start all over. Go ahead and finish your printing plate. Just be careful at the places where it is torn.

After inking the plate, remove the paint at the torn spot with a cotton swab. However, if the tear ruins an important detail of your drawing, such as an eye in a portrait, you have no choice but to start again from the beginning.

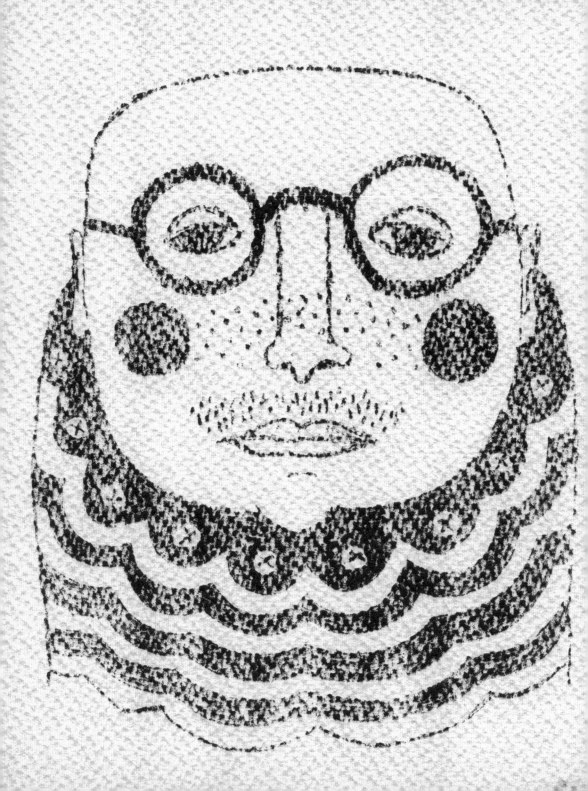

RIGHT AND WRONG PAPER

Generally speaking, you can print on all types of paper. Depending on which kind of paper you choose, you should consider a few things.

If you want to print on very thin paper (for example, tissue paper), make sure to remove the excess water on the printing plate with a paper towel after inking it. Be especially careful when you peel off the paper from the printing plate after the print process. The paper will have soaked up water from the printing plate and can easily tear. Thin paper will also become especially wavy when drying.

With thick paper or even cardboard you need to apply more pressure when printing. If you use too little pressure, your print will probably be very light. Make sure to increase the pressure only slightly, though, because too much pressure can break the glass plate underneath the aluminum foil.

Paper with a rough texture, such as handmade paper, can result in an uneven print image, because the paint does not reach all parts of the drawing evenly. To reduce this effect, apply more paint and use more pressure on the paper during printing.

FUZZY PRINT IMAGE WITH MULTICOLOR PRINTING

When making a multicolor print with two or more printing plates, some of the paint from the first printing plate can rub off from the paper onto the aluminum foil of the second plate, and that plate will then absorb paint in those places the next time it is inked, resulting in a fuzzy print.

You can try to wipe off these spots with a wet sponge after each inking. If that doesn't help, give the prints enough time to dry before you continue with the next printing plate.

If you apply gum arabic to the plates, you can easily wipe off paint from areas that should remain blank with a wet sponge after inking the plate. Go to page 86 in the chapter "Additional Techniques" to learn how to apply gum arabic.

Due to the water on the printing plate, your paper can become wavy. This makes it more difficult to place the paper accurately on the printing plate during the second or third printing. You can either let the paper dry and then press it smooth or you can remove the water from the printing plate after each inking.

ADDITIONAL TECHNIQUES

GUM ARABIC

Applying gum arabic is not necessary to achieve good print results. However, it can be a great help for beginners. Inserting this step, we created our first printing plates that led to crisp, clean print results.

Gum arabic makes your printing plate tougher. The aluminum foil gets a protective layer, which makes it stronger. This way you can also print larger runs without a problem.

The technique is easy. Prepare your printing plate and ink it as explained in steps 1 through 5. Then put a teaspoon of gum arabic on the printing plate and spread it with a brush over the entire surface, including the drawing. You will now see how the gum arabic adheres to all the places that will remain unprinted later. The areas that will be printed repel the gum arabic.

Usually, it takes a few hours for the gum arabic to dry. Once the protective layer is completely dry, you can begin printing.

Gum arabic is collected from the bark of various species of the acacia tree. In painting, it is used as a binding agent of paint pigments. In its liquid state, it is repelled by the oil–based paint, and it becomes solid when it dries. Gum arabic can be found in fine art supply stores.

You can speed up the drying process of gum arabic by using a hairdryer. You can blowdry the printing plate relatively quickly on a cool setting.

If you aren't sure whether the gum arabic is completely dry, touch it lightly with your finger on the edge. If a fingerprint is left in the gum arabic, you should wait a little longer.

ALUMINUM FOIL WITH TEXTURE

Some of the aluminum foil you find in supermarkets has a honeycomb structure, which is supposed to make it more tear–resistant. You can also use this type of aluminum foil to create a printing plate, as long as you do not mind the honeycomb pattern, which will show up in your print because the paint sticks to the raised parts in the structure.

Try integrating the honeycomb structure into your design. For example, here we picked it up for the sweater pattern.

TRACING

If you prefer to play it safe and don't want to draw on your plate freehand, you have two options to trace a template onto your prepared printing plate.

CARBONLESS PAPER

The first option is working with carbonless paper. Start by preparing a drawing on paper. Remember that it must be a mirror image of your design.

Then take your prepared printing plate, place the carbonless paper on it and your drawing on top of that. With a hard, sharp pencil, trace the lines of your drawing, applying light pressure. Then trace the resulting outlines on your printing plate with an oil–based pencil and fill in any solid areas with a soapy brush.

TRANSPARENT PAPER

The second option is using transparent paper. Prepare your drawing on the transparent paper and place it on the prepared printing plate. With a hard pencil or pen, trace the lines of your template, applying light pressure. This creates slight impressions of your drawing on the aluminum plate, which you can then trace with an oil–based pencil.

This technique is particularly helpful if you want to make a multicolor print with several printing plates. Using this method, you can draw each planned printing plate on a sheet of transparent paper and place them on top of one another to ensure that everything matches up perfectly.

Carbonless paper usually has a layer of wax that is transferred directly to the printing plate during tracing. This means that you can choose to proceed directly with etching rather than tracing the drawing on the plate with oil–based pencil. This works especially well if you want to print very fine lines. Make sure to check first that the traced lines are transferred fully and consistently.

If you are working with transparent paper, you do not need to draw a mirror image of your design. Simply place the side with the drawing facing downward and trace it from the back.

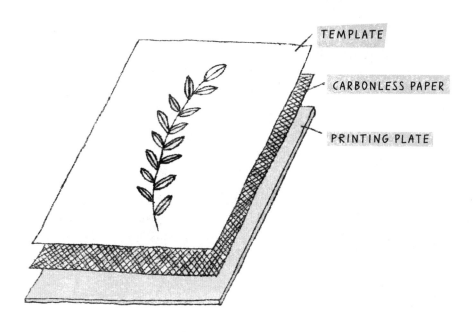

TEMPLATE

CARBONLESS PAPER

PRINTING PLATE

PRINTING PLATE

LARGE FORMATS

Even though a roll of aluminum foil only has a certain width, you can still print larger formats. We are presenting three methods here.

MULTIPLE PRINTING PLATES ON ONE FORMAT

If you want to print a 22–by–34–inch poster, for example, you can create eight letter–sized printing plates and print them in sequence on your poster. Working together with another person makes it much easier to arrange the large paper on the printing plate. However, with this method it is difficult to print a single design in a large format.

1. DRAWING ON THE ALUMINUM FOIL

2. ETCHING

3. INKING

4. PRINTING

PRINTING IN THE TUB

For the second method, you need a tiled surface. Since you will be creating your printing plate on this surface, it is important that cola and water can flow out below. That is why a bathtub is perfect for this.

The tiles should be clean and smooth. Moisten them with water, roll out a sheet of aluminum foil, and cut it to the desired length. The foil will stick to the tiles due to the water. Now you can draw your design on the aluminum foil and proceed to etching.

Because the cola flows down quickly when you are working vertically, you need more of it here; about four cups should be enough.

The structure of the tiles will show up in the print. We like the effect this creates. However, if you would rather do without the tile look, you may prefer the third method, explained on the next spread.

In the spring when the barbecue season begins, many supermarkets carry very strong and wide aluminum foil, which is perfectly suited for working with large formats. The aluminum foil we used here is about 16 inches wide.

PRINTING ON A WINDOW

We tested the third method of printing large formats, which requires a large, smooth surface, on the glass window of our balcony door. To catch the cola, oil, and water that run out below, we placed a long planter in front of the door.

Here, too, start by moistening the surface with water. Roll out a sheet of aluminum foil and cut it to the desired length. We let the aluminum foil go all the way into the planter. Now take a second roll of aluminum foil and roll it out next to your first sheet, slightly overlapping it. Repeat this until your printing plate has the desired width. Then draw your design on the aluminum foil and proceed with the next steps.

PRINTING ON WOOD AND FABRIC

Paper is not the only material you can print on with this technique. The printing process remains the same as described earlier in this book. The only thing different is the material on which you are printing.

On the following pages, we will show you two other possibilities besides paper.

YOU CAN EVEN PRINT
ON BALLOONS. SEE PAGE 110.

PRINTING ON WOOD

Wood is a pretty good material for printing. However, you should make sure that your printing plate is saturated with paint. You also have to apply more pressure than with paper.

If you want to print on a thick piece of wood, remove the inked aluminum foil from the plate and carefully position it on the wood surface. Then rub your finger over the aluminum foil until all parts of your drawing have been transferred equally to the wood.

1. POSITIONING

2. SMOOTHING OUT WRINKLES

3. APPLYING PRESSURE WITH HANDS

4. CAREFULLY PEELING OFF FABRIC

PRINTING ON FABRIC

To print on fabric, you should also keep a few things in mind. When placing the fabric onto the prepared printing plate, it is important to stretch it a bit, so that it doesn't wrinkle. Once the fabric is on the printing plate, make sure it doesn't shift or pucker. You can try smoothing out the fabric on the plate with a roller or a spoon. However, if you notice that the fabric is shifting, just press it down with your hands. Remove the fabric from the printing plate very carefully. As long as the paint is moist, the design can still distort.

The paint needs more time to completely dry on the fabric. After a week, you can wash the printed fabric at a cold temperature in the washing machine.

THIS IS HOW WE DID IT:

LABELS → 14

To make the labels, we drew several different designs directly on one printing plate. This way we ended up with multiple labels on the printed sheet, which we then only had to cut out and stick on. We attached some of the labels with twine.

CARDBOARD BOXES → 18

First, we assembled the boxes. Then we prepared the printing plate with the design and, after inking it, removed the aluminum foil from the glass plate. Finally, we carefully placed the aluminum foil on the desired spot on the box and pressed it on with our fingers. It was helpful here to work as a pair.

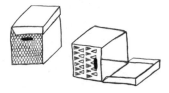

PAPER BAGS → 16

To print the paper bags, we removed the excess water on the inked printing plate with some paper towels before printing. On our first attempt the design came out a little blurred, because there were two layers of paper between the roller and the printing plate. We then tried using the roller on the inside of the bag, which worked great! Using the same printing plate, we then also printed envelopes.

POSTCARDS → 19

We used three printing plates for the postcards. One for the colorful areas, one for the black lines, and another one for the back of the postcard, which includes a place marker for stamps.

For double-sided printing, make sure to place a sheet of paper between the roller and the printed paper so that the back is not stained during printing.

POSTERS → 20

Our glass plates were too small to print a large-sized poster, so we used an old plexiglass plate from a light box on which to roll out the aluminum foil. Since the printing plate was now too large to etch it in the sink, we performed this step in the tub. The posters were printed in three colors in three passes.

GARLANDS → 22

For the shape of the pennants we cut out a template and drew it on the printing plate. Then we drew the patterns into the shapes and printed them. This made it easier for us to cut out the pennants in the right size later on.

NOTEBOOKS → 23

For the notebook covers, we used beautiful, colorful cardboard paper, large enough to fold over the back. We only printed on the front. Once the covers had dried, we folded them in the middle and sewed them to the interior with thread-stitching. Then we cut the notebooks to the right size with a cutting machine.

BUTTONS → 24

For the buttons we borrowed a small button-making machine. To make sure the printed designs would not be cut off at the edges later, we included a bleed of .125 inches. Here, too, we printed several designs on a letter-sized sheet of paper, then cut out circles, and assembled all the button parts with the button machine.

STICKERS → 25

To make the stickers, we used conventional adhesive label paper from the craft store. We prepared a printing plate with different designs, which we then printed on letter–sized sticker paper. Since the sticker paper is very thin, it rolls up after printing. Therefore, we pressed the printed sheets between two paper towels in a thick book.

After the prints were dried and pressed, we cut out the individual designs. This way you can quickly produce small runs of stickers.

ART PRINTS → 26

Over time we have made a lot of prints. Instead of just letting them collect dust in a drawer, we framed them and created a nice picture wall.

WOODEN TRIVETS → 28

We bought wooden boards at the hardware store and cut them to the desired size. Then we prepared and inked the printing plate. Since the wood is quite thick, we carefully removed the inked aluminum foil from the glass plate and placed it directly on the wooden trivet. This made it easier to transfer the print to the wood.

WOODEN MAGNETS → 29

We printed the magnet designs on pieces of wood of different thicknesses. With the thin pieces of wood, we printed several motifs on one sheet of wood by placing it directly on the printing plate and pressing it firmly to the plate. Then we cut out the individual circles.

For the thicker magnets, we used round pieces of wood that we then printed on individually. Since the wood was quite thick, we removed the aluminum foil from the glass plate and placed it directly on the wood for printing. This way we were able to exert more pressure than on the glass plate and could better transfer the print to the wood.

SHIRTS → 30

We placed a thin piece of cardboard inside the shirt at the place where it was to be printed. Then we pulled the fabric tightly over the edges of the cardboard so there would be no wrinkles. We put the shirt on the prepared printing plate and rolled over the cardboard with a roller, pressing it firmly to the plate to transfer the drawing. With this technique, you can print on both light and dark fabric, but simple designs work better than detailed drawings with thin lines.

PILLOW COVERS → 32

Many pillow covers are made of thick fabric. Based on our experience, it is better to print monochromatic designs on such materials, since the print often comes out relatively light. Darker colors also work better than lighter ones here.

TOTE BAGS → 34

We positioned the tote bags on the inked printing plate and then applied pressure on the inside of the bag with a roller. This leads to a better print quality than using the roller on the back of the bag.

ART PRINT ON FABRIC → 33

This art print on fabric was made using eleven different printing plates, which we arranged freely during the print process, without planning or register marks.

DISHTOWEL → 37

Dishtowels usually have a very rough and uneven structure. We applied a generous amount of paint to the printing plate to make sure the print would not come out too light. We then placed the dishtowel on the printing plate and rolled over it lightly with the roller to smooth out a few wrinkles.

Since the roller can quickly pucker the fabric when it rolls over it, we then applied pressure with our fingers and the balls of our hands. If you use dark paint, you can see through the fabric where you need to press down on the dishtowel to transfer the drawing (see also page 104).

STREET ART → 98–99

For the paste–up, we prepared a "printing plate" on the window of our balcony door. We first printed out the design on several pieces of letter–sized paper, which we assembled to create a template in the original size. Then we transferred the design to the aluminum foil and proceeded to etching and printing. To make a second print in another color, we taped register marks to the window for both the template and the paper on which we printed (see also pages 96–97).

BALLOONS → 101

We printed on the inflated balloons. Since balloons can slip easily on a wet printing plate, we dabbed up excess water from the inked printing plate with a paper towel. Then we placed the balloon on the edge of the design and rolled it over the drawing until it had touched all parts of it.

ABOUT US

We are Lucas and Laura, two designers and illustrators from Darmstadt, Germany. We met at the Darmstadt University of Applied Sciences while studying communication design. Since 2015 we have been working together as Studio Lula, designing and printing lots of wonderful things. The joy we get from experimenting has often led us down unexpected and exciting paths.

We also offer workshops for all those who want to give working with their hands a try, feel like experimenting, or simply want to make some beautiful prints.
Come visit our website.

www.studio-lula.com

THANKS

Émilie Aizier–Brouard, thank you very much
for inventing this printing technique, which has
become so very dear to our hearts!

A special thanks to Bertram and Karin
Schmidt–Friderichs, Brigitte Raab, Isabell Henninger,
and all the nice publishing people who worked
on this book.

A huge thank you to Armin Brenner and
Markus John of the type foundry New Letters
for the wonderful font Tilde.

A big hug and eternal gratitude to Addi, Alex,
Anka, Eva–Lotta, Hanna, Heike, Ina, Ingo,
Joachim, Jonas, Jonathan, Katharina, Knut, Lena,
the Löwentor team, Marvin, Mathes, Micha,
Michael, Nadja, Rebecca, Silvie, Sina, Tonio,
Vroni, and Waltraud.

IMPRINT

Princeton Architectural Press
A McEvoy Group company
37 East 7th Street, New York, NY 10003
202 Warren Street, Hudson, NY 12534
Visit our website at www.papress.com.

First published in Germany with the title
In unsrer Küche wird gedruckt by
Verlag Hermann Schmidt.
© 2016 Verlag Hermann Schmidt and the authors

English edition
© 2017 Princeton Architectural Press
All rights reserved
Printed and bound in China
20 19 18 17 4 3 2 1 First edition

Concept, illustrations, photos, and text:
Laura Sofie Hantke and Lucas Grassmann
Design: Laura Sofie Hantke and Lucas Grassmann

Lithography and final artwork:
Laura Eckes, Isabell Henninger

Typeset in Tilde
(designed by Armin Brenner and Markus John,
www.new–letters.de)

For Princeton Architectural Press:
Translator: Jane Wolfrum
Project editor: Nicola Brower
Typesetting: Mia Johnson

Library of Congress Cataloging–in–Publication Data
Names: Hantke, Laura Sofie, author. |
    Grassmann, Lucas, author.
Title: Kitchen lithography : hand printing at home :
    from buttons and bags to postcards and pillowcases /
    Laura Sofie Hantke, Lucas Grassmann.
Other titles: In unserer Küche wird gedruckt.
English Description: English edition. | New York :
    Princeton Architectural Press, 2017. | "First published
    in Germany with the title *In unsrer Küche wird
    gedruckt* by Verlag Hermann Schmidt."
Identifiers: LCCN 2017004097 | ISBN 9781616896232
    (alk. paper)
Subjects: LCSH: Lithography—Technique.
Classification: LCC NE2430 .H2713 2017 |
    DDC 763—dc23
LC record available at https://lccn.loc.gov/2017004097